Drawing Fun

HOW TO DRAW

Flowers

by Kathryn Clay

illustrated by June Brigman

Capstone press

Mankato, Minnesota

Snap Books are published by Capstone Press,
151 Good Counsel Drive, P.O. Box 669, Mankato, Minnesota 56002.
www.capstonepress.com

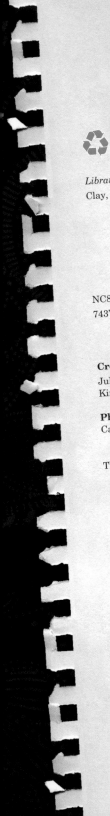

Books published by Capstone Press are manufactured with paper
containing at least 10 percent post-consumer waste.

Library of Congress Cataloging-in-Publication Data
Clay, Kathryn.
    How to draw flowers / by Kathryn Clay; illustrated by June Brigman.
    p. cm. — (Snap books. Drawing fun)
    Includes bibliographical references and index.
    Summary: "Lively text and fun illustrations describe how to draw flowers" — Provided by publisher.
    ISBN: 978-1-4296-3403-8 (library binding)
    1. Flowers in art. 2. Drawing — Technique. I. Brigman, June. II. Title. III. Series.

NC815.C53 2010   2009006649
743'.73 — dc22

Credits
Juliette Peters, designer
Kim Brown, colorist

Photo Credits
Capstone Press/TJ Thoraldson Digital Photography, 4 (pencil), 5 (all), 32 (pencil)

The author dedicates this book to Andy, Shelly, Jennie, and Marty.

Table of Contents

Getting Started

Check out most art museums, and you're bound to see a few flower paintings. Because flowers come in a variety of shapes, sizes, and colors, they provide endless inspiration for artists. Now it's your turn to create a floral masterpiece.

Maybe you want to draw blossoms bursting with color? Then take a look at the bright red poppy. Do you love delicate designs? Then check out the tiny flowers on a lily of the valley. If you prefer drawing traditional flowers, try sketching a single red rose.

You won't find every flower variety in this book. After all, there are thousands of different types of flowers! But once you've mastered some of the flowers here, you'll be able to draw all kinds of beautiful bouquets. Put your inner florist to work, and see what flower designs you can draw.

Must-Have Materials

1. First you'll need something to draw on. Any blank, white paper will work well.

2. Pencils are a must for these drawing projects. Be sure to keep a bunch nearby.

3. Because sharp pencils make clean lines, you'll be sharpening those pencils a lot. Have a pencil sharpener handy.

4. Even the best artist needs to erase a line now and then. Pencil erasers wear out fast. A rubber or kneaded eraser will last much longer.

5. To make your drawings pop off the page, use colored pencils or markers.

Carnation

Roses may be the most popular flower, but carnations are a close second. Carnations are long-stemmed flowers with ruffled petals. Their dainty petals make these flowers perfect for corsages.

Try drawing a fancy corsage. Start with a carnation. Then add baby's breath, mini roses, and a ribbon.

STEP 1

STEP 2

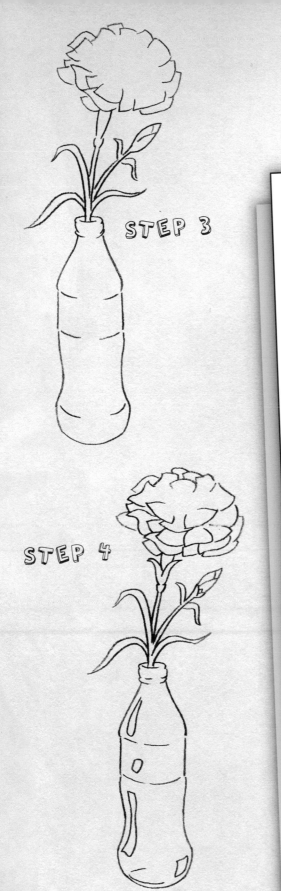

STEP 3

STEP 4

Daisy

Daisies are hardy flowers that can grow just about anywhere. That's why these familiar flowers are sometimes considered weeds. To draw these wildflowers, start with a round center. Then add lots of skinny petals.

Try drawing a field of wild daisies blowing in the wind.

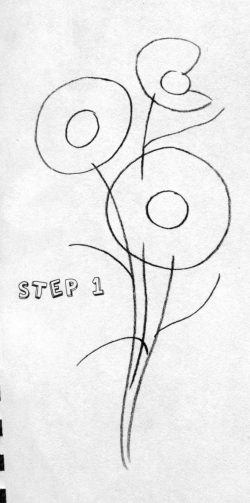

STEP 1

STEP 2

STEP 3

STEP 4

Hydrangea

Bees are always buzzing around giant hydrangea (hi-DRAIN-juh) blossoms. Hydrangeas are flowering shrubs filled with clusters of tiny flowers. Each small flower has four petals. Together these flowers can form blossoms up to 8 inches (20 centimeters) wide.

After drawing one hydrangea, try drawing an entire shrub full of blossoms.

STEP 1

STEP 2

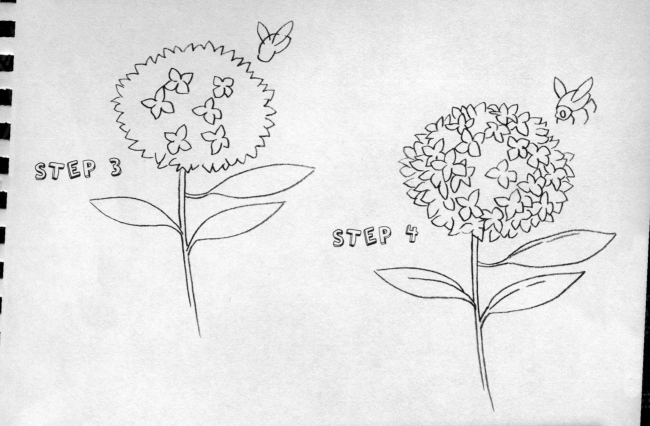

STEP 3

STEP 4

Lily

Lilies are easy-to-grow flowers that add a blast of color to gardens or bouquets. A stargazer lily, like the one here, has bright pink petals with white tips. Some lilies, like the tiger lily, have orange petals and black spots.

Try drawing a bouquet of tiger lilies.

STEP 1

STEP 2

STEP 3

STEP 4

13

Lily of the Valley

Lily of the valley has small, bell-shaped flowers surrounded by pointy, green leaves. This flower blooms in early spring. Its sweet smell attracts all kinds of birds and butterflies.

Draw a butterfly resting on a lily leaf.

STEP 1

STEP 2

STEP 3

STEP 4

15

Poppy

Wild poppies grow in giant fields that can be seen from miles away. Most people think of poppies as being a bright red color. But their paper-thin petals can also be white, pink, or purple.

Once you've mastered one poppy, try drawing a field filled with poppies.

STEP 1

STEP 2

STEP 3

STEP 4

Tulip

Tulips are prized for their unique styles. Some people even spend thousands of dollars on hard-to-find tulip varieties. For a basic tulip, draw a thick stem and a single flower with six petals. Then add long, waxy leaves.

Try creating your own tulip variety. Do the petals have pointed tips or ruffled edges?

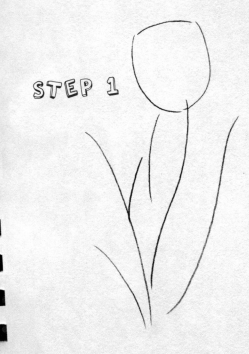

STEP 1

STEP 2

STEP 3

STEP 4

Snapdragon

Snapdragons are unusual flowers with an even stranger name. Each stem has a cluster of small flowers that resemble a dragon's mouth. Squeezing the sides of this snout-shaped flower creates a snapping sound.

Draw a window box filled with red, yellow, and pink snapdragons.

STEP 1

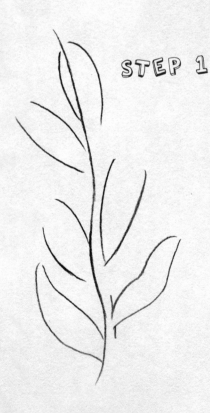

STEP 2

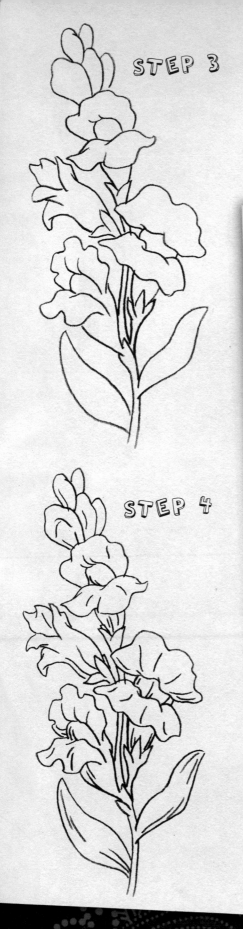

STEP 3

STEP 4

21

Sunflower

Sunflowers tower over other plants. At 3 to 10 feet (1 to 3 meters), they're some of the tallest flowers. And because sunflowers symbolize loyalty, they are perfect flowers to draw for your best friend.

Once you've drawn a sunflower, try drawing a bird snacking on the seedy center.

STEP 1

STEP 2

STEP 3

STEP 4

Rose

You've heard that roses are red. But they're also white, pink, yellow, orange, and purple. With all those colors, it's easy to see why roses are a florist favorite. This rose includes a barely-there bud, a full-blown blossom, and a few thorns, of course.

After drawing one rose, try drawing a bouquet of multi-colored roses in a tall vase.

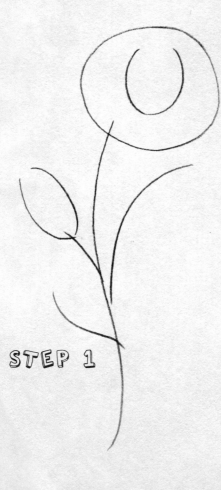

STEP 1

STEP 2

STEP 3

STEP 4

Flower Garden

Now that you've practiced several flowers, try drawing them together as one colorful garden. Start with a big hydrangea bush. Add a few tulips, daisies, carnations, poppies, and snapdragons. Then draw a fence to keep your garden safe from pests.

Maybe you love pansies or hollyhocks. Try drawing a garden filled with all of your favorite flowers.

STEP 1

STEP 2

STEP 3

To finish this drawing, turn to the next page. ⟹

STEP 4

STEP 5

28

Glossary

bouquet (boh-KAY) — a bunch of picked or cut flowers

corsage (kor-SAHJ) — a small flower bouquet worn on clothing or strapped to the wrist

florist (FLOR-ist) — someone who sells flowers and plants

hardy (HAR-dee) — able to survive in poor weather

inspiration (in-spihr-AY-shun) — something that fills someone with an emotion, an idea, or an attitude

symbolize (SIM-buh-lize) — to stand for or represent something else

Read More

Clay, Kathryn. *How to Draw Cute Animals*. Drawing Fun. Mankato, Minn.: Capstone Press, 2010.

Harpster, Steve. *Pencil, Paper, Draw! Flowers*. New York: Sterling, 2008.

Whittle, Janet. *How to Draw Flowers in Simple Steps*. Tunbridge Wells, Kent: Search Press Limited, 2008.

Internet Sites

FactHound offers a safe, fun way to find Internet sites related to this book. All of the sites on FactHound have been researched by our staff.

Here's all you do:

Visit *www.facthound.com*

FactHound will fetch the best sites for you!

Index